I like to Whine!

by William G. Bentrim

BEARLY TOLERABLE

© 2009

PUBLICATIONS

Author's Note

As a former teacher, guidance counselor and current parent and grandparent, I am distinctly cognizant that as far as kids go, there are no experts. Expertise is based on experience and learning. We may learn out of the same books but each and every one of us have different experiences with our own families.

Kids whine, good kids and kids that aren't so good, they all whine. Many times their intent isn't to whine and sometimes that is exactly what they intend. Whining isn't indicative of a "bad" kid. It is normal. Normal doesn't make it any easier to listen to, day in and day out. If this book, aimed at preschoolers, can even slow down some of the whining, it will be a monumental contribution to parental mental health.

Hopefully it will make your child smile and perhaps you too, can smile seeing the normalcy of their behavior. If nothing else, this book may help you to appreciate how good your own child really is.

Dedicated to all the wonderful children I have had in my life and to those I have yet to meet.

William G. Bentrim

You can't make me stop watching TV, cried PeeWee!

Not listening to parents don't you see, means in the future No TV!

I don't want to clean my room!
It's not fair!
I can't find anything to wear!
It's your fault not mine,
Jean whined.

A messy room
in which you live
can make you crazy,
but it isn't your
parents fault if
you are lazy!

I want more cake, cried Jake.
I want to eat until I have a belly ache!

You are what you eat, too many sweets and you'll end up barfing on your feet.

I don't wanta go for a ride, whined Clyde.

Whining about what you don't want to do, generally means your parents won't listen to you.

6

I don't want to stop picking my nose.
I don't care if it's gross to you.
I'll do what I want to do!

Sometimes it seems Mom and Dad aren't fair, but for them to be wrong is usually rare.

I don't wanna go to bed, whined Fred!

A kid who doen't get rest, will never grow up to be best.

I don't wanna sit in my car seat, screamed Pete!

Obeying the law is always the best. If your parents don't use the car seat they will be under arrest.

Bill took my ball, wailed Paul. I don't want to play if I can't have my own way!

If in all things you have your own way,
you won't have any friends by the end of the day.

I want to go to the monster show, cried Moe.

Whining to go is a sure way to see that you won't go no matter how important the show.

Waa! I want candy, screamed Andy!

Crying for stuff
is always bad.
Crying when hurt is ok
with Mom and Dad.

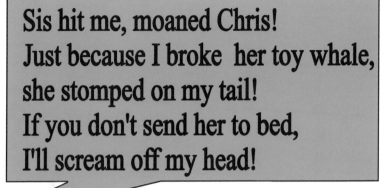

Sis hit me, moaned Chris!
Just because I broke her toy whale,
she stomped on my tail!
If you don't send her to bed,
I'll scream off my head!

Breaking a toy because
you didn't get your way,
makes sure you won't
be allowed to play.
Hurting another even
when they are bad,
will end up making
you feel sad.

Waa! I dropped my ice cream, cried Eileen! I want more now or I'm going to stomp my feet and get red as a beet!

Screaming and stomping the feet will never, ever, get you a treat.

14

I'm not lying, lied Ryan.
I didn't do it.
You can't prove it.
It wasn't my pen, it must
have been my friend.

Kids do things wrong,
parents understand
but to lie and to shout
means getting a time out.

I ordered pizza pie,
now I don't know why.
If you make me
eat it, I know I'll just cry!

It's ok to change your mind
but crying and whining
isn't the way to get
what you want on any day.

I won't share my toy, cried Joy.

Sharing toys with others
you might not want to do,
but if you don't share your toys
who will share with you?

The wise old owl says,
getting your own way
seems to be normal today.
Spoiled is the direction you'll go
unless you're lucky enough
to have folks who say NO!
Whining doesn't make you glad,
whining just makes you sad.
Why not be glad?
Listening to Mom and Dad,
just isn't so bad!

The End

Activities

With a reading age child, read the story with the child being the wise old owl and the parent being the whining child. The parent should discuss with the child how they felt listening to the parent whine.

The parent should whine about several things and ask the child to react as the parent. This exercise provides insight as to how the child perceives the parental response and also enables the child to see how annoying whining is.

Parent and child should establish a whining signal. It can be one finger in the air or a shake of the head, whatever the parent and child can agree to use. When a child starts to whine, the parent can use the signal. The signal is for the child to stop their whining and think about what they are saying and how they can make their point without whining.

The parent may wish to provide a reward for developing self control. Keep it simple, a lollipop or a special treat or 15 minutes of TV, something tangible that allows the child to perceive the benefits of developing better self control.

Parents can log actual whines from their children and then read the book using actual whines and their own solutions. The purpose of the book is to promote interaction between parent and child and to abridge a behavior pattern before it becomes a lifelong habit.

Log actual whines and then address those whines at a later time and show the child how their behavior has changed for the better.

Behavior can be changed through discussion and interaction. Parents should give the child a set quantity of something the child values. This could be pennies, chocolate kisses, marbles, just something the child perceives as valuable. Establish a location where the item can be placed as a penalty each time the child whines. At the end of the week, sit down and see how many pennies out of 100 the child has left. Discuss the progress the child has shown and let them keep what ever remains of the set quantity. Do this on a weekly basis until the child sees a relation-ship between behavior change and rewards.

Perhaps the hardest activity will be for the parent to carefully lis-ten to their own interaction with others to determine whether they are whining as well. Children often emulate their parents, both the good and the bad traits.

Keep in mind that your children most likely will outgrow whining but your involvement may make it a less lengthy and annoying process.

Happy Parenting!